D1129371

THE
COLLECTED ARTICLES
OF CLAUDE MCKAY

By

CLAUDE MCKAY

Read & Co.

Copyright © 2021 Read & Co. Books

This edition is published by Read & Co. Books,
an imprint of Read & Co.

This book is copyright and may not be reproduced or copied in any
way without the express permission of the publisher in writing.

British Library Cataloguing-in-Publication Data
A catalogue record for this book is available
from the British Library.

Read & Co. is part of Read Books Ltd.
For more information visit
www.readandcobooks.co.uk

CONTENTS

CLAUDE MCKAY

By Robert Thomas Kerlin

An English subject, being born and growing to manhood in Jamaica, Claude McKay, a pure blood , was first discovered as a poet by English critics. In Jamaica, as early as 1911, when he was but twenty-two years of age, his *Constab Ballads*, in Negro dialect, was published. Even in so broken a tongue this book revealed a poet—on the constabulary force of Jamaica. In 1920 his first book of poems in literary English, *Spring in New Hampshire*, came out in England, with a *Preface* by Mr. I. A. Richards, of Cambridge, England.

Meanwhile, shortly after the publication of his first book, he had come to the United States.

Here he has worked at various occupations, has taken courses in Agriculture and English in the Kansas State College, and has thus become acquainted with life in the States. He is now on the editorial staff of the Liberator, New York.

There has been no poet of his race who has more poignantly felt and more artistically expressed the life of the American Negro. His poetry is a most noteworthy contribution to literature.

From Spring in New Hampshire I am privileged to take a number of poems which will follow without comment:

SPRING IN NEW HAMPSHIRE

Too green the springing April grass,
   Too blue the silver-speckled sky,
For me to linger here, alas,
   While happy winds go laughing by,
Wasting the golden hours indoors,
Washing windows and scrubbing floors.

Too wonderful the April night,
   Too faintly sweet the first May flowers,
The stars too gloriously bright,
   For me to spend the evening hours,
When fields are fresh and streams are leaping,
Wearied, exhausted, dully sleeping.

THE LYNCHING

His spirit in smoke ascended to high heaven.
His Father, by the crudest way of pain,
Had bidden him to his bosom once again;
The awful sin remained still unforgiven:
All night a bright and solitary star
(Perchance the one that ever guided him,
Yet gave him up at last to Fate's wild whim)
Hung pitifully o'er the swinging char.
Day dawned, and soon the mixed crowds came to view
The ghastly body swaying in the sun:
The women thronged to look, but never a one
Showed sorrow in her eyes of steely blue,
And little lads, lynchers that were to be,
Danced round the dreadful thing in fiendish glee.

THE HARLEM DANCER

Applauding youths laughed with young prostitutes
And watched her perfect, half-clothed body sway;
Her voice was like the sound of blended flutes
Blown by black players upon a picnic day.
She sang and danced on gracefully and calm,
The light gauze hanging loose about her form;
To me she seemed a proudly-swaying palm
Grown lovelier for passing through a storm.
Upon her swarthy neck, black, shiny curls
Profusely fell; and, tossing coins in praise,
The wine-flushed, bold-eyed boys, and even the girls,
Devoured her with eager, passionate gaze:
But, looking at her falsely-smiling face,
I knew her self was not in that strange place.

IN BONDAGE

I would be wandering in distant fields
Where man, and bird, and beast live leisurely,
And the old earth is kind and ever yields
Her goodly gifts to all her children free;
Where life is fairer, lighter, less demanding,
And boys and girls have time and space for play
Before they come to years of understanding,—
Somewhere I would be singing, far away;
For life is greater than the thousand wars
Men wage for it in their insatiate lust,
And will remain like the eternal stars
When all that is to-day is ashes and dust:
But I am bound with you in your mean graves,
Oh, black men, simple slaves of ruthless slaves.

Distinction of idea and phrase inheres in these poems. In them the Negro is esthetically conceived, and interpreted with vision. This is art working as it should. Mr. McKay has passion and the control of it to the ends of art. He has the poet's insight, the poet's understanding.

Perhaps the most arresting poem in this list, and the one most surely attesting the genius of the writer, is *The Harlem Dancer*. It is an achievement in portrayal sufficient by itself to establish a poetic reputation. The divination that penetrates to the secret purity of soul, or nobleness of character, through denying appearances—how rare is the faculty, and how necessary! Elsewhere I give a poem from a Negro woman which evinces the same divine gift in the author, exhibited in a poem no less original and no less deeply impressive—Mrs. Spencer's *At the Carnival*. Here I will companion *The Harlem Dancer* with one from Mr. Dandridge, for the comparison will deepen the effect of each:

ZALKA PEETRUZA
(Who Was Christened Lucy Jane)

She danced, near nude, to tom-tom beat,
With swaying arms and flying feet,
'Mid swirling spangles, gauze and lace,
Her all was dancing—save her face.

A conscience, dumb to brooding fears,
Companioned hearing deaf to cheers;
A body, marshalled by the will,
Kept dancing while a heart stood still:

And eyes obsessed with vacant stare
Looked over heads to empty air,
As though they sought to find therein
Redemption for a maiden sin.

'Twas thus, amid force-driven grace,
We found the lost look on her face;
And then, to us, did it occur
That, though we saw—we saw not her.

Returning to Mr. McKay, we may assert that his new volume of verse, Harlem Shadows, confirms and enhances the estimate of him we have expressed.

A CHAPTER FROM
Negro Poets and Their Poems, 1923

THE COLLECTED ARTICLES OF CLAUDE MCKAY

SOCIALISM AND THE NEGRO

Published in
Workers' Dreadnought,
31 January 1920

Chiefly through the efforts of Dr Dubois, author of *The Souls of Black Folk*, there came into being in the United states, some ten years ago the National Association for the Advancement of Coloured People. In the main the organisation strode to combat the insidious influence of Booker Washington, who, making light of the social and political status of his race, had put into practice, for its material benefit, the principle of work advocated by Carlyle. A group of wealthy and socially and politically influential bourgeois of the North helped to launch the movement and became its directing spirit.

In it were men and women representative of the old conservative and Quaker aristocracy of New England and Pennsylvania, and the liberal capitalists. It comprised intellectual and commercial Jews, and its finest spirit was Oswald Garrison Villard, editor of the *American Nation* and grandson of the great Abolitionist, who, vilified and denounced by the hide-bound capitalist press, stands out as the solitary and only consistent representative of the American bourgeoisie, counselling peace and moderation between aggressive Capitalism and its government and Militant Labour and Socialism, and all the forces of passion struggling in America today. This group palpably ignorant of the fact that the Negro question is primarily an economic problem, evidently thought it might be solved by admitting Negroes who have won to wealth and intellectual and other attainments into white society on equal terms, and by protesting and pleading to the political and aristocratic South to remove the notorious laws limiting the political and social status of coloured folk. So far as I am able to judge, it has done good work on the technically legal and educational side. It developed race-consciousness in the Negro and made him restive; but on the political side it has flirted with different parties and its work is quite ineffective.

Further it has taken a firm stand against segregation, which is a moot and delicate question. While all Negroes are agreed that the social barriers must be removed, there is much difference as regard to education and some institutions like hospitals and churches. The growing number of cultured Negro men and women find it extremely difficult to obtain employment that is in keeping with their education under the capitalist system of government. For one instance, had a scholar like Dr. Dubois been white he would certainly have secured a chair at Harvard, Yale or Columbia University, for which he is eminently fitted. Many negroes have obtained a sound education at great sacrifice, only to be forced upon completion of their studies, into menial or uncongenial toil. In the black belt of New York City, where there is an estimated population of 100,000 Negroes, the Police Force, hospital, library and elementary schools—patronised chiefly by coloured people—are entirely manned by white staffs. It would be impossible for such conditions to exist under a soviet system of Government.

Just about the beginning of the late War, the Socialists and the I. W. W., realising that the Negro population offered a fertile field for propaganda, began working in earnest among them. With the aid of the *Messenger Magazine*, edited by two ardent, young Negro university men, and *The Liberator*, they have done a real constructive work that is now bearing fruit. The rank-and-file Negroes of America have been very responsive to the new truths. Some of them have been lured by the siren call of the American Federation of Labour to enter its ranks. For years this reactionary association held out against Negro membership, but recently the capitalist class, alarmed over the growth of revolutionary thought amongst the blacks, used its creature, Gompers, to put through a resolution admitting Negroes to membership at the last conference. It has, however, had no effect on the lily-white and inconsequential trade unions of the South.

A splendid result of the revolutionary propaganda work among the blacks was the Conference of the National Brotherhood of Workers of America (entirely Negro) which was held in Washington, D. C., in September last year. Its platform is as revolutionary in principle as that of the I. W. W. Over 100 delegates were in attendance and the majority came from the South. As always, the coloured workers are ready and willing to meet the white workers half way in order that they might unite in the fight against capitalism; but, owing to the seeds of hatred that have been sown for long years by the master class among both sections, the whites are still reluctant to take the step that would win the South over to Socialism. The black workers hold the key to the situation, but while they and the whites remain divided the reactionary South need not fear. The great task is to get both groups together. Coloured men from the North cannot be sent into the South for propaganda purposes, for they will be lynched. White men from the North will be beaten and, if they don't leave, they will also be lynched. A like fate awaits coloured women. But the South is boastful of its spirit of chivalry. It believes that it is the divinely-appointed guardian of sacred white womanhood, and it professes to disenfranchise, outrage and lynch Negro men solely for the protection of white women.

It seems then that the only solution to the problem is to get lovely and refined white women to carry the message of Socialism to both white and black workers. There are many of them in the movement who should be eager to go. During the period of Reconstruction a goodly number went from New England to educate the freed men and, although they were socially ostracised by the Southerners, they stood to their guns. To-day they are needed more than ever. The call is louder and the cause is greater. Among the blacks they will be safe, respected and honoured. Will they rise to their duty?

Strangely, it is the professional class of Negroes that is chiefly opposed to Socialism, although it is the class that suffers and complains most bitterly. Dr Dubois has flirted with the socialist idea from a narrow opportunist-racial standpoint; but he is in spirit opposed to it. If our Negro professionals are not blindly ignorant they should realise that there will never be any hope— no sound material place in the economic life of the world—for them until the Negro masses are industrially independent. Many coloured doctors, lawyers, journalists, teachers and preachers literally starve and are driven to the wall because the black working class does not earn enough to give them adequate support. Naturally, the white workers will hardly turn from their kind to coloured aspirants to the professions, even though the latter should possess exceptional ability. And even when they are capable they are often up against the prejudices of their own people who have been subtly taught by the white ruling class to despise the talented of their race and sneer at their accomplishments.

During the War, Marcus Garvey, a West Indian Negro, went to New York and formed the Universal Negro Improvement Association, and African Communities League for the redemption of Negro Africa. The movement has had an astonishing success. Negroes from all parts of the world, oppressed by the capitalists, despised and denied a fighting chance under the present economic system by white workingmen, have hailed it as their star of hope, the ultimate solution to their history-old troubles. It now numbers over two million active members. The capitalist press which ridiculed it at first now mentions the Association in flattering terms, especially since it successfully floated the Black Star Line Steamship Company. At the beginning the company had much trouble with the local authorities, but it has never been persecuted by the State of Federal Government, for it is non-Socialist of course. Although an international Socialist, I am supporting the movement, for I believe that, for subject peoples, at least, Nationalism is the open door to Communism. Furthermore, I will try to bring this great army of awakened workers over to the finer system of Socialism. Some English Communists have remarked to me that they have no real sympathy for the Irish and Indian movement because it is nationalistic. But today the British Empire is the greatest obstacle to International Socialism, and any any of its subjugated parts succeeding in breaking away from it would be helping the cause of World Communism. In these pregnant times no people who are strong enough to throw off the imperial yoke will tamely submit to a system of local capitalism. The breaking up of the British Empire must either begin at home or abroad; the sooner the strong blow is struck the better it will be for all Communists. Hence the English revolutionary workers should not be unduly concerned over the manner in which the attack should begin. Unless, like some British intellectuals, they are enamoured of a Socialist (?) British Empire! Unless they are willing to be provided with cheap raw materials by the slaves of Asia and Africa for the industries of their overcrowded cities, while the broad, fertile acres of Great Britain are held for hunting and other questionable pleasures.

Claude McKay

THE
CAPITALIST WAY:
LETTOW-VORBECK

Published in
Workers' Dreadnought,
7 February 1920

Lettow-Vorbeck, who commanded the German forces in East Africa during the late War, has written a story of their campaign. For the English rights of publication he is paid a tidy sum by British interests. Journalism has become a favourite pastime for the German junkers who have lost their jobs for the moment, and, let us hope, permanently. Ludendorf and Tirpitz have earned good money in America by their pens, and we may expect a flood of apologies and memoirs from the discredited Imperialists of Germany and Austria-Hungary.

For the English version of this useless mass of printed stuff, the American and British Empire workers pay directly. But, perhaps, the masses like to read what these bloody murderers have got tell of their orgies of blood spilling.

We must pay tribute to the far-seeing policy of International Capitalism in noting how its press buys these books, reviews them favourably, and thus gives the writers a chance to live comfortably until their dark days are over. The capitalists soon forgive each other their mistakes. It is we workers who keep on hating each other on account of race differences, nationality and colour! We workers! we do not forgive so easily. And it is to the interests of our masters that we should not!

But back to Lettow-Vorbeck and his East Africa campaign. In

his story, he tells of the exploits of his black troops, how faithful they were, how courageous and skilful under fire. England also used her black troops, and the whole nasty business shows to what depths Capitalism will descend to maintain its supremacy. Ignorant black men were pitted against their brothers to fight for a cause that was alien to them.

May-be, the exploiting class have not considered the fact that if the blacks have fought so well for an inglorious purpose, they might fight yet better, when properly led and thoroughly aroused, for the economic and social rights, of which they are deprived in their native land.

In the Capitalist league, Smuts has inserted a clause to prevent the natives being trained to the use of firearms. Time will show whether the secret arming of the negroes can be prohibited. The eyes of the Negroes all over the world are turned to South Africa, where the blacks are living under conditions that are more intolerable than those existing in the Southern states of America. South Africa, to-day, is a potential powder plant, which at any moment, may be blown up by the least spark of fire. The Negro delegates will go home from England to tell their people that the British Government can do nothing to remove the unjust restrictions that retard their social and economic progress. This news will only help to intensify the deep hatred existing between the white and black workers, not to mention the spirit of rebellion that is now being fostered by all negroes subject to British Imperial rule. The *Negro World*, published in New York City, informs its numerous readers in Africa, the West Indies and the Americas of everything of interest that goes on amongst coloured people in every part of the globe. Happily, the policy of the Anglo-Saxon abroad, unlike English diplomacy at home, is driving coloured peoples of all classes and all shades into One Big Union of Revolt.

From the Johannesburg *International* we glean the fact that Capitalism, through one of its organs, is demanding the removal of the colour bar. And it will be abolished if it is inimical to the selfish interests of the exploiters! Such an event would, doubtless, make the natives grateful to their real oppressors, while the cleavage between them and the white workers would become greater. It is the duty of South African Socialism, if it be genuine, to forestal any such action, or, if it is helpless in the matter, to prove to the natives, by propaganda, that the revolutionary white workers, who are making the fight for freedom, are with them in their struggle for justice.

In the January *Liberator*, Mary White Ovington, a woman of the Southern aristocracy, we think, declares that the brutalities practiced upon coloured people would be stopped at any time the Southern oligarchy willed it. This clear fact has long been apparent to all close observers of the strife between the races.

The exploiting classes will set black against black, white aginst black, and face right about, if necessary to keep their power. If for nothing more than sheer self-preservation, it is of great moment, now, that the white and coloured workers should get together, to find a real basis of mutual agreement and co-operation in the industrial world.

Socialism should step in to bridge the gulf which has been created between white and coloured workers by Capitalism and its servant, Christianity. There is plenty of work to be done, and no time should be lost, for who knows when the storm will break?—when rivers of blood will flow, bearing the souls of white and black workers into eternity? Then, perhaps, the Anglo-Saxon world will wake up to find, all at once, a thousand Amritsars on its hands!

CLAUDE MCKAY

A BLACK MAN REPLIES

Published in
Workers' Dreadnought,
24 April 1920

DEAR EDITOR: The following letter, replying to E. D. Morel's article on the black troops in Germany, was sent to the *Daily Herald* on April 11th, but apparently the *Herald* refuses a hearing to the other side, which is quite inarticulate:—

THE EDITOR OF THE *Daily Herald*.

SIR: The odiousness of your article headlined "Black Scourge in Europe; Sexual Horror let loose" is not mitigated by your explanatory editorial and note stating that you are not encouraging race prejudice and that you champion native rights in Africa. If you are really consistent in thinking that you can do something to help the white and black peoples to a better understanding of each other, there is much you might learn from Liberal and Conservative organs like *The Nation, The New Statesman* and the *Edinburgh Review*, which have treated the problem (exposing the iniquities practised on the natives and showing up the shortcomings of the latter) in a decent and dignified matter.

Your correspondent, who peddles his books and articles on "the poor suffering black", is quite worked up over the African warriors carrying off the prizes of war like the heads and eyes of their victims. But, verily, trophies of war are trophies of war whether they are human works of art like paintings and sculpture or nature's like man's hands and heads. I am quite ignorant of the "well-known physiological reasons that make the raping of a white woman by a negro resultful of serious and fatal injury". Any violent act of rape, whether by white, yellow or black, civilised or savage man, must entail injury, serious or fatal, especially if the victim is a virgin. The worst case of rape I ever heard of took place in Kansas City some eight years ago; the woman was white, the perpetrators three white men, and the result was well-nigh fatal. In the West Indies there have been many instances of white soldiers raping coloured women with awful consequences. Your correspondent employs the same methods used by the German propagandists during the war without any real effect. England, France, even America, all used their black troops in the war. Surely the *Daily Herald*, by the light of experience, ought to find a more effective and honest way of combating a great evil.

Why all this obscene, maniacal outburst about the sex vitality of black men in a proletarian paper? You might say the negro is over-sexed; the same statement may be made of the Italians or Jews of the Caucasian race. To say the black man is "sexually unrestrainable" is palpably false. I, a full-blooded negro, can control my sexual proclivities when I care to, and am endowed with my fair share of primitive passion. Besides I know of hundreds of negroes of the Americas and Africa who can do likewise. When white men go among coloured races they do not take their women with them; hence the hundreds of mulattos, octoroons, and eurasians disowned by the Caucasian race.

During my stay in Europe, I have come in contact with many weak and lascivious persons of both sexes, but I do not argue from my experience that the English race is degenerate. On the other hand I have known some of the finest and cleanest types of men and women among the Anglo-Saxons.

If the black troops are syphilitic it is because they have been contaminated by the white world. According to competent white investigators, syphilis is a disease particular to white and yellow peoples; where it is known amongst the blacks it has been carried thither by the whites. Houses of prostitution have always been maintained, officially or otherwise, for soldiers. They were a notorious fact during the late war. I think the key to your exposure may be found in your extract from *Clarté*, which states "German women of barely marriageable age sell themselves because 20 francs are worth 150 marks, and 50 francs 400 marks." In this intolerable age the great majority of peoples, male and female, in different ways are given to prostitution. The stopping of French exploitation and use of the North African conscripts (not mercenaries, as your well-informed correspondent insists they are) against the Germans is clearly a matter upon which the French Socialists should take united action. But not as you have done.

I do not protest because I happen to be a negro (I am disgusted when I read in your columns that the white dockers would prohibit their employers using Chinese and Indian labour). I write because I believe the ultimate result of your propaganda will be the further strife and blood-spilling between the whites and the many members of my race, boycotted economically and socially who have been dumped down on the English docks since the ending of the European War. I have been told in Limehouse, by white men, who ought to know, that this summer will see a recrudescence of the outbreaks that occurred last year. The negro-baiting Bourbons of the United States will thank you, and the proletarian underworld of London will certainly gloat over the scoop of the Christian-Socialist-pacifist *Daily Herald*.

Yours etc.

CLAUDE MCKAY

REVIEW OF
CREATIVE REVOLUTION

Published in

Workers' Dreadnought,

July, 1920

BOOK REVIEW: *Creative Revolution* by Eden and Cedar
Paul (1920)

The authors of this book tell us that Creative Revolution is
an endeavour to clear much prevalent confusion away from the
path of socialist theory, but it is likewise a call to arms, and so on.
It would seem that the work was chiefly written for
revolutionary leaders and propagandists especially those of an
artistic temperament. The writers think that "The Dictatorship
of the Proletariat" should be superseded by a newly-coined word
"Ergatocracy" and the first chapter is a definition of it and its
underlying principles. "Ergatos", it is explained, is the Greek
word for "worker". The term seems so unfortunate; it savours of
autocracy and suggests a smile when one thinks of "ergo". But it
might go into the language like ochlocracy—mob rule—without
ever becoming popular like democracy.

The chapter on Social Solidarity is primarily address to
bourgeois intellectuals. It deals principally with Bertrand
Russell (who, by the way, puts Ethel Snowden in the shade in
his polite attack on the Russian Communists in the Nation of
10th inst.) Ramsay McDonald and the Fabians. One gathers
from it that while this gang would endeavour to capture
parliament, and institute a reformist rule of labour, the workers

should concentrate on the destruction of Parliament and the substitution of "regional and occupational soviets."

In The Class Struggle the work of the Plebs League and Labour Colleges, the Syndicalists and the I.W.W. is lightly touched upon. Towards the end of the chapter we find the pronouncement: "We do not build too much on the possibilities of corrupting the armed forces of the Crown. There are other methods for ensuring the victory of the workers when the decisive moment comes." But somewhere else the authors hint at the perils and hardships that a revolution in England might bring to the workers from her utter dependence on foreign countries for food. Such suffering would become unbearable, if a loyalist Navy controlled the trade routes and America and the great Colonies remained reactionary, and would inevitably result in an abortive revolution which might lead to a subsequent period of inaction and reaction. It seems that, as was done in Russia, some efficient means must be devised to disseminate propaganda among the highly-organised and trustworthy fighting forces of the world, unless the "other methods for ensuring the victory of the workers" are made known, tried and deemed feasible.

In appraising the Shop Stewards' movement, the authors declare that "we have no Lenin here, nor need of one"; a rather odd thing to say when, as Communists and Revolutionaries, we are always slating our official leaders for betrayal of the cause. Personally, I do not care what class the English Lenin comes, but I am sure it will require an iron will to mould the efficient minority that must carry on the work of the revolution during the transition stage.

The book is well prepared and it runs the gamut modernist literature from Whitman, Marx and Morris to Freud, Jung and Trotsky.

The quotations are copious This from Rosa Luxemburg's Revolutionary Socialism is very fine:—

"To-day we can seriously set about destroying Capitalism once and for all . . . If the proletariat fails to fulfil its duty as a class, we shall crash down together in the common doom." There is another, exceedingly good, from Direct Action by Willie Gallacher and J. B. Campbell:—

"The workers have to create organisations to counter the State organisation of capitalism. The joint industrial and social committee should be the nucleus of working-class political power. As the industrial and social organisation grows strong enough it will be forced to fight the Capitalist State, not to take possession of, but to smash it."

But there are also a strangely-involved passages like this which is apparently meant to explain the principle:—

"As Communist ergatocracy realises itself in practice; as the socialist mentality becomes generated under Socialist institutions; when the ownership rule, which is the essential characteristic of bourgeois democracy, has been destroyed beyond all possibility of revival; when the government of men has been replaced by the administration of things—then, with the passing of the phase of the dictatorship of the proletariat, the connotation of the "cracy" element of the term ergatocracy, will suffer a sea-change."

REVIEW OF FIRST PRINCIPLES OF WORKING CLASS EDUCATION

Published in
Workers' Dreadnought,
11 September 1920

The author has presented to proletarian students a simple lucid and comprehensive treatise based on the Marxian interpretation of human life and labour, which should be read by every studious and thinking worker. It should find its way into all working-class colleges, classes, clubs, libraries and homes.

In spite of its simplicity, the book calls for careful study; there are many excellent diagrams and no headway can be made in the reading and digesting of the contents without carefully consulting them. A thorough perusal of the first chapter, Historico-Sociological, will give the reader the necessary understanding of the method that Clunie employs throughout the text in giving visual form to his investigations. The worker in any given branch of industry will find herein, by a critical perusal and study of the diagrams, in what relation his industry stands in relation to all other, how each is linked up to each and skilfully manipulated by the controlling interests to serve their own selfish purposes.

Perhaps the simplest illustration is on page 11, but one may add much to it in the imagination. It gives a clear cut division between the exploiting classes, what might almost be a split from the very top to the lowest strata of our society; and right down along the line of on the one side is to be seen, active or passive, the worker-supporters of the Capitalist regime, the retainers of the robber lords, even the harpies of the slums, the vicious element which Engels says somewhere, will willingly become the instruments of the counter-revolution to fight against the revolutionary will of the class-conscious proletariat. The difference is not so marked here, on account of the individualistic or anti-social tendency of the British workers; but on the Continent, where the co-operative movement is essentially working-class, untainted by petit-bourgeois contact as it is in England, the division is quite noticeable in the social life of the workers.

The index chapter deals exhaustively with the status of Labour in the existing social order. It shows how orthodox, or Trade Union, labour is by reason of its growth and strength, reactionary and reformist, and naturally antagonistic to Revolutionary Labour. But because of the extension of Capital and pressure from the Revolutionary Labour, Trade Unionism is reluctantly pushed into revolutionary channels. The recent development in the Trade Union movement here lend added interest to this chapter.

On page 14 there is a clear and definite statement which should help to enlighten and comfort idealistic Socialists who often find it impossible to to work and hold intercourse with their fellows of the same faith, because their conduct often belies their Socialist principles: "The connection between man and man is not a human but a property relationship, and will remain so until society is really humanised, and this cannot be until their material relationship has become socialised universally."

A keen observation of the remarkable diagram on objective economics, which, making use of unscientific terms, shows the powerful hold that "dead" capital has upon "living" labour. The subsequent chapters, dealing with value, exchange value, exchange, surplus value and wages will richly reward the diligent reader in search of lucid information on matters that are of especial interest in these times of tumbling exchange and chaos in international commerce. They would doubtless help to enlighten many bourgeois economists of the Harold Cox school of thought.

But perhaps the most illuminating thing in the book is the short chapter xi, that takes up the "nature and function of Capital." It is beautifully clear, and ends with a brief, brilliant summary. The appendix is useful, especially the sections dealing with American banking concerns, and giving a list of epoch-making inventions of the world. Altogether an excellent book.

'First Principles of Working Class Education price 8s 6d post free 9s 6d By James Clunie, Socialist Labour Press, 50 Renfrew Street Glasgow.

COMMUNISTS
AND THE LOCAL
COUNCILS OF ACTION

Published in
Workers' Dreadnought,
25 September 1920

I think it is of vital importance that Communists as such, should seek representation in the local Councils of Action. When Comrade Whitehead argues that "the action contemplated is industrial action, the people who are going to act are industrial workers," he is merely presupposing a beautiful syndicalist dream that has no reality in our world of capitalist domination. If the industrialists of a council were to formulate and act upon a "down tools" policy only, that would merely be a demonstration of protest against the exploiting class. In the ensuing struggle should the industrialists win, they would immediately have to decide upon an "up tools" policy, and take over the social work of administration that was formerly done by the expropriating class. It matters not that industrialists may be appointed to carry out the new duties of distribution, exchange and community welfare work. The moment they accept the appointments, they are no longer industrialists, but community workers or politicians. Communists should note clearly the difference— and there is a vast difference—between industrial (productive and distributive) and social (useful and necessary) work that is not rooted in the Trade Unions, workshop or factory, although it derives its strength therefrom.

Comrade Whitehead beclouds the issue and misinforms

us when he states that "the action contemplated is industrial action," and leaves it at that. It was the making of an industrial weapon *for a political purpose, viz.*, to stop an open war against Russia. It is self-evident that the British workers wouldn't stand for another great war—they were willing to lend their industrial strength to their political Labour leaders to prevent an act that would have affected them vitally, but the moment the danger seems to be passed they become apathetic. The war against Russia still goes on, but the mass mind of the workers is as callous about it as it is towards Ireland's martyrdom. While Whitehead advocates Communist abstemption from the local councils (except as industrialists), he wants to SOVIETISE THE COUNCILS OF ACTION.

If, as Communists we accept the Russian Soviet principle, we should clearly understand that the local Soviets do not exclude non-industrialists. (1) The local soviet is made up of all useful workers, Red Army and Peasants' Deputies. (2) The City Soviet takes its members from *a.* the factory; *b.* the Union; *c.* political parties; *d.* (with the workers' consent) individual candidates; *e.* the military. The Dictatorship of the Proletariat which is one of the conditions of membership of the Communist Party is clearly the political expression of the industrial workers. What Comrade Whitehead advocates is the very negation of communism, Sovietism, the Communal or Community Life. It is syndicalism pure and simple—a form of industrialism that some proletarian Anarchists who require economic backing like to flirt with. But even some of the French pioneers of this movement have come to realise that Syndicalism is not enough, that under modern conditions of life it would be unworkable, and the Bolsheviks are urging the French Communists to fight the syndicalists.

Communists who ignore the local Councils of Action are making a big mistake. Where are our eyes and our vision? These Councils are the nuclei of the British Soviets, which it is the bounden duty of Communists to enter and transform from

Trades Councils into All Workers' Councils. In our local districts we should form Leagues and Societies and seek admission to the local council in whatever way we can. We should endeavour to get the ex-servicemen on the councils. It is more effective to get inside and act than to criticise from without. Criticism of the National Council is unnecessary and beside the mark. We all know that it is the creature of the Labour Party and Trade Union Officialdom. It is not a National Council. But it is up to the local councils to destroy it in the interests of the Revolution.

THE
REVOLUTION
IN CURRENCY

Published in
Workers' Dreadnought,
9 October 1920

At the moment of writing, the Capitalist nations of the world, and the bankrupt nations, Germany, Austria, Hungary and Bulgaria, are met in conference at Brussels, to find new ways and means of carrying on the rapidly failing business of international trade and finance. The big international financiers who dwelt in a fool's paradise during the war, gambling excessively and rioting in the enormous surplus wealth produced by the sweat and blood of the working-class, are now panic-stricken, being faced with a worldwide breakdown of credit and finance.

Do British working men realise that the great Eastern lands contain vast stores of commodities which cannot be exchanged for lack of controlled and regulated trading power and liquidation in Western lands? Still, while the granaries and warehouses of the East are overflowing with raw materials, the proletariat there is ground down in poverty.

While Russia has solved the problem by a sweeping system of socialisation, the Continent, endeavouring to bolster up the old rotten structure, is practically bankrupt, and a revolution in currency, affecting the entire world, is going on in the keenly competing capitalist countries—England, Japan and America. In the latter country, the only remaining one which still maintains a gold standard of circulation, credit currency has risen from 25 billions dollars before the war to 70 billions dollars at the present day. Actual paper money has increased from 7 to 50 billions, while the gold reserve is but 7 billion dollars—an increase of one billion over the pre-war quantity. Because of the backwardness of organised labour in America, and the apparent stability of the Capitalist system, that country might comparatively easily depreciate her currency to the point where commodities can appreciably be expressed in terms of gold. This policy, however, would involve a certain dislocation and readjustment of industry, with a consequent decrease in accumulated capital, which the government dare not face.

The Battle Between London and New York,

On the other hand, England is indebted to the United States for over £865,000,000, which daily tends to grow greater, as the exchange rates move against this country. The National floating debt is 50 per cent. more than the foreign. The annual interest that the workers of England must pay on this huge foreign debt, practically amounts to more than what can be paid off yearly in instalment on the principal. We must pay this debt in goods or gold. We haven't enough of the first to give, for we can no more obtain cheap raw materials on long terms of credit. And much what we might give America would not care to take. Hence the insistent demand of the American financiers for gold payments.

This urgent demand creates a panicky feeling in banking circles in London, for it is plainly an American bid and threat to have the financial centre of the world, the gambling mart, transferred from London to New York. The workers of England should guess what lies in store for them, between these two opposing forces, if they do not effect the social revolution here before the crisis comes to a head.

The Labour Party's Policy,

Among other things, the Labour Party urges a deflation of the currency, and a League of Nations' international loan to meet the exigences of the situation. Close observers of the financial and labour world should know that a quiet deflation of the currency has been in operation for weeks—a fortnight ago, over half a million pounds currency notes was withdrawn from circulation within a week—resulting in thousands of workers being forced out of employment. And an international loan is improbable as, barring the United States, no country can afford to lend very much. The Labour Party has no international policy. It flouts Moscow, the real heart of Internationalism to-day, but it has nothing to offer us. Winston Churchill was right when he said: "Labour was not fit to govern." The Labour Party thinks it can solve international problems by mouthing Christian platitudes through the columns of the *Daily Herald*. Its chief point, depreciating the currency in terms of gold, to bring down prices, is worthless. It would certainly bring distress and disorganisation to the working class, and make commodities cheaper only for the the already wealthy classes. The production of gold has diminished by 27 per cent. during the last decade, whilst the metal as expressed in commodities, has been reduced to nearly 50 per cent. of its pre-war value. No-one knows how much more valueless gold, in spite of its scarcity, might become in proportion to the necessities of life. It were better for revolutionaries if the value should keep on decreasing.

The Gold Standard Destroyed,

The gold basis of commodities in Europe is destroyed for ever. If it be maintained in America, it can work little harm to the rest of the world, if we establish Soviets in all of Europe. In the different countries, Government bonds have taken the place of money currency for the international exchange of goods: international exchange is regulated either by goodwill in currency or barter. There is a Continental school, which would try and stabilise the currency as it is, opposed to a conservative British school that hankers after the dead order of things. Behind the Continental school, centred in France, is a group of big British financiers, on whose strength the French gamblers (so that they may continue their military exploits), buy and sell the English pound on the American market, thus keeping the exchanges in an ever-fluctuating state.

The Slave States of Germany and Central Europe,

Such is the condition of Central Europe, on account of the White Guards' activities, that the workers there can hardly work, but are reduced to a despairing rabble. And our German bothers and sisters deprived of their productive machinery, are toiling in virtual slavery for the French gamblers. This is the chaos that the International Capitalists and their bourgeois servants are trying to straighten out in Brussels, a the expense of the workers of the world.

The Jingo Capitalists are solely responsible for the terrible plight of the working people of the world to-day. Yet our wretched masters appeal to the crude patriotism of the workers and try to fix the blame on the war, the Germans and the Jews. Belgium, which was overrun by the German hordes, is on the Capitalist road to prosperity. Even Northern France, in spite of the brazen militarism of her Imperialists, is in a fair way of rehabilitation. But Germany, which was not devastated, cannot get on her feet—nor can Central Europe. Why? For the vital instruments of production, tonnage, rolling-stock and coal, have been wrested from them by the Allied Capitalism, which lacks the necessary material, equipment and capacity to us the looted machinery for needful productive purposes. The workers of Germany and Central Europe are now helpless slaves and the slaves of the Allies are exhorted to toil harder and harder to feed and clothe their victimised fellow-workers of the Continent, and the thousands of black and white soldiers that the Allies maintain in the occupied areas to prevent Germany and central Europe adopting the Soviet system of government—the only way out of the capitalist chaos that the workers can choose. The capitalist drones proclaim the Word of Humanity and the harlot church, the prostitute press and the little labour leaders parrot the pious lie: "More production in the old way", which means keener competition and greater exploitation of labour. That is the concern of Capitalism for Humanity.

We may sit by and sat that it is too late, the system cannot be saved. But it may survive in another form. It is for the workers to destroy it. Japan, America, and England are waging grim war against each other. The Japanese are successfully capturing British trade in India and other Eastern lands. America is selling in Britain manufactures and food-supplies cheaper than the British can produce and sell these things to their own people. All these nations are seeking to exploit the backward peoples of Asia and Africa to secure cheap raw materials and cheap labour, which will enable them to dictate the terms of working-class existence to their own proletariat.

The cry of the labour leaders, bourgeois humanitarians and financial experts like Sir George Paish, for the workers to increase output to save Europe, is a false alarm. There was a great increase in production during the war, when millions of men were taken from productive work to slaughter each other. Under Governmental bureaucracy, new industries of destruction were created to win the war, and millions of pounds and rich securities were put into the bulging pockets of the capitalists. After the war, many of these worthless industries were favoured by the Government for the sole benefit of the employers, although it was pretended that this was done to absorb the ex-service men. Soldiers and non-combatants came

41

back from the war in millions to purchase life's necessaries with inflated government notes, while engaged in unnecessary work. The Capitalists retain and seek larger profits, with the resultant economic conditions facing the world to-day. Visitors to Germany and Central Europe, declare that there is an abundance of food, luxuries and delicacies in these countries, which only the very wealthy can procure. The poor working-classes, which are absorbing the middle-class, are starving. The acute distress in food and housing conditions is entirely due to the monstrosity of the capitalist system. Russia is the only country which grappled successfully with the matter; and she could only achieve success by a drastic system of socialisation. By abolishing the old money system and establishing commercial relations based on goodwill and co-operation, she will attract all the countries of the East to her. Russia's triumph will bring a great new life to all the workers of the world. Her way is the only way for Western nations to follow. Any other way will only bring defeat and destruction to the cause of the workers.

THE YELLOW
PERIL AND THE DOCKERS

Published in
Workers' Dreadnought (16 October, 1920)
under the pseudonym Leon Lopez

A fortnight ago three friends and I went down to the West India docks to visit a ship that had just arrived from the Argentine. It was not an unpleasant morning, the air was crisp, there was a slight wind and the bus ride was quiet pleasant. But when we reached the docks, there was no feeling of happiness prevailing there. There were hundreds of dockers loitering along the wharves waiting for a chance to work. There were scores upon scores of seamen, white, brown and black, waiting wistfully for an undermanned ship. Despair was written in great large letters all over their faces: still they waited, hope against hope. We almost forgot our own pressing troubles as we made our way through the pitiful body of strong men, willing, eager to sell themselves to the merciless and intrenched employers for bread: yet refused a chance to toil on the docks that are stored with fine cloth and good food, while their wives and children are in rags and starving.

We were met at the gate by an old pal who took us down to the hold of his ship, where we had breakfast à la creole, rice and corn meal and flour dumplings, swimming in coconut oil and thick coarse unadulterated cocoa made in native style with fat floating on the top. It was a great meal and for years I had not tasted one like it; but it turned bitter in my mouth when I thought of the despairing crowd of men outside. Even the wretched life of my swarthy friends in the ships' bottoms was better than gnawing starvation ashore.

My friend, Pedro, did not hear any news of his people in Brazil and he too was ina state of despair as he could not secure a berth to work his way back home. I came back west wondering what steps would be taken to relieve the awful distress in docklands. I did not wonder for long. A few evenings after, a Harmsworth-Northcliffe news-sheet blazoned the remedy from its posters all over London:

CHINATOWN SCANDAL
WHITE GIRLS AND YELLOW MEN
POPLAR COUNCIL APPEAL TO HOME OFFICE

There was some excitement in the West India Dock Road. Mr Cairns and the Evening News had turned the trick. For the first time in many hopeless weeks, the jobless dockers and seamen would forget their hunger to vent their wrath on the Chinamen and the other coloured elements in Poplar. The next evening I visited the West India Dock Road to see what was happening. And business was going on as usual in one of the large Chinese restaurants, there was the usual number of white girl waitresses — quite pretty some of them. In light banter, I put the question to them that I have often asked before: "Why do you work here?" the answer is: "The pay is better than what we can get in the West End, the tips are large and our petty Chinese masters are kinder than our big ghoulish bosses." In some restaurants, the white mothers sit with their quaint half-caste babies. The kept Press, with an air of mock innocence, asks: "What fascination do our English girls find in these coloured foreigners?" The kept Press ought to know, when its position is the same as the girls', with the sole difference that its wages is higher and the prostitutes are men. The great food firm of Lyons', with its long chain of restaurants scattered all through London, is determined to drive hundreds of its striking girls to a worse life than that of Chinatown, because they tried to organise themselves into a Union. And Lyons pay the Press to do their dirty work.

I tried my luck on a Chinese lottery and lost my 2/-, but it was harmless; I felt much safer than I could in a West End gambling den. If one is partial to the pipe and can present credentials, one may rest at ease on a mat and smoke in peace and at leisure in some back room in Chinatown. There is an exotic flavour in Dockland, and existence would not be intolerable there were it not for the hideous spectre of unemployment which haunts the wharves and which must be laid at the door of English Capitalism.

A few months ago the dockers got a rise in wages, and English ships soon vanished from English ports. In Liverpool, Hull, Bristol and Cardiff, conditions are just as bad. The British ships are being diverted to continental ports where labour is cheaper. This affects skilled labour of all trades. As well as the great mass of unskilled workers.

The whole plot is so obvious and yet the nicely fed and clothed labour officials play the capitalist game to perfection, by stirring up the passions of the workers against aliens (need I add Jews?) At Portsmouth, last month, the Ships Stewards and Cooks Union put through a resolution "protesting against the employment of all Chinese and Asiatic labour, requesting the Government to repatriate all Chinese not of British nationality, and asking that in future no Chinese be engaged on board British ships west of the Suez Canal." Since the beginning of last year, the Government has gone far towards meeting these demands and standardising the rate of pay; but the seamen officials do not believe in a standard wage for all ship workers. One of them informed me recently, that the black men had been organised, and the Indians were being brought into line, but the Chinese were hopeless! They will not live and work up to the general standard of British seamen and if the standard of wages were ever so high, the ship-owners would use the Chinese as their tools and potential scabs against the white. Therefore only one course is open: Chinese must must not be employed on British ships, nor allowed to reside in English ports. As I have seen Chinese working and living just like other people in different parts of the world, I know that the premise is false. The dockers, instead of being unduly concerned about the presence of their coloured fellow men, who like themselves are the victims of capitalism and civilisation, should turn their attention to the huge stores of wealth along the water front. The country's riches are not in the West End, in the palatial houses of the suburbs; they are stored in the East End, and the jobless should lead the attack on the bastilles, the bonded warehouses along the docks to solve the question of unemployment.

HOW BLACK
SEES GREEN AND RED

Published in
The Liberator, Vol. 4 No.6
July 1921

LAST summer I went to a big Sinn Fein demonstration in Trafalgar Square. The place was densely packed, the huge crowd spreading out into the Strand and up to the steps of the National Gallery. I was there selling the Workers' Dreadnought, Sylvia Pankhurst's pamphlet, Rebel Ireland, and Herman Gorter's Ireland: The Achilles Heel of England; I sold out completely. All Ireland was there. As I passed round eagerly in friendly rivalry with other sellers of my group, I remarked aged men and women in frayed, old fashioned clothes, middle aged couples, young stalwarts, beautiful girls and little children, all wearing the shamrock or some green symbol. I also wore a green necktie and was greeted from different quarters as "Black Murphy" or "Black Irish." With both hands and my bag full of literature I had to find time and a way for hearty handshakes and brief chats with Sinn Fein Communist and regular Sinn Feiners. I caught glimpses also of proud representatives of the Sinn Fein bourgeoisie. For that day at least I was filled with the spirit of Irish nationalism-although I am black!

Members of the bourgeoisie among the Sinn Feiners, like Constance Markievicz and Erskine Childers, always stress the fact that Ireland is the only "white" nation left under the yoke of foreign imperialism. There are other nations in bondage, but they are not of the breed; they are colored, some are even Negro.

It is comforting to think that bourgeois nationalists and patriots of whatever race or nation are all alike in outlook. They chafe under the foreign bit because it prevents them from using to the full their native talent for exploiting their own people. However, a black worker may be sensitive to every injustice felt by a white person. And I, for one, cannot but feel a certain sympathy with these Irish rebels of the bourgeoisie.

But it is with the proletarian revolutionists of the world that my whole spirit revolts. It matters not that I am pitied, even by my white fellow-workers who are conscious of the fact that besides being an economic slave as they, I am what they are not-a social leper, of a race outcast from an outcast class. Theirs is a class, which though circumscribed in its sphere, yet has a freedom of movement—a right to satisfy the simple cravings of the body—which is denied to me. Yet I see no other way of upward struggle for colored peoples, but the way of the working-class movement, ugly and harsh though some of its phases may be. None can be uglier and harsher than the routine existence of the average modern worker. The yearning of the American Negro especially, can only find expression and realization in the class struggle. Therein lies his hope. For the Negro is in a peculiar position in America. In spite of a professional here and a business man there, the maintenance of an all-white supremacy in the industrial and social life, as well as the governing bodies of the nation, places the entire Negro race alongside the lowest section of the white working class. They are struggling for identical things. They fight along different lines simply because they are not as class-conscious and intelligent as the ruling classes they are fighting. Both need to be awakened. When a Negro is proscribed on account of his color, when the lynching fever seizes the South and begins to break out even in the North, the black race feels and thinks as a unit. But it has no sense of its unity as a class-or as a part, rather, of the American working-class, and so it is powerless. The Negro must acquire class-consciousness. And the white workers must accept him and work with him, whether they object to his color and morals or not. For his presence is to them a menacing reality.

American Negroes hold some sort of a grudge against the Irish. They have asserted that Irishmen have been their bitterest enemies, that the social and economic boycott against Negroes was begun by the Irish in the North during the Civil War and has, in the main, been fostered by them ever since. The Irish groups in America are, indeed, like the Anglo-Saxons, quite lacking in all the qualities that make living among the Latins tolerable for one of a conspicuously alien race. However I react more to the emotions; of the Irish than to those of any other whites; they are so passionately primitive in their loves and hates. They are quite free of the disease which is known in bourgeois; phraseology as Anglo-Saxon hypocrisy. I suffer with the: Irish. I think I understand the Irish. My belonging to a subject race entitles me to some understanding of them. And then I was born and reared a peasant; the peasant's passion for the soil possesses me, and it is one of the strongest passions in the Irish revolution.

The English, naturally, do not understand the Irish, and the English, will not understand unless they are forced to. Their imperialists will use the military in Ireland to shoot, destroy and loot. Their bourgeoisie will religiously try to, make this harmonize with British morality. And their revolutionists-I would almost say that the English revolutionists, anarchists, socialists and communists, understand Ireland less than any other political ,group. It appears that they would like to link up the Irish national revolution to the English class struggle with the general headquarters in England. And as Sinn Fein does not give lip-service to communism, the English revolutionists are apparently satisfied in thinking that their sympathy lies with the Irish workers, but that they must back the red flag against the green.

And the Irish workers hate the English. It may not sound nice in the ears of an "infantile left" communist to hear that the workers of one country hate the workers of another. It isn't beautiful propaganda. Nevertheless, such a hatred does exist. In the past the Irish revolutionists always regarded the Royal Irish Constabulary as their greatest enemy. Until quite recently its members were recruited chiefly from the Irish workers themselves; but the soldiers of the Irish Republican Army shot down these uniformed men like dogs, and when at last thousands of them deserted to Sinn Fein, either from fear of their fighting countrymen, or by their finer instinct asserting itself, they were received as comradeship, fed, clothed and provided with jobs. I saw one of the official Sinn Fein bulletins which called upon the population to give succor to the deserting policemen. They were enemies only while they wore the uniform and carried out the orders of Dublin Castle. Now they are friends, and the British have turned to England and Scotland for recruits. And so all the hatred of the Irish workers is turned against the English. They think, as do all subject peoples with foreign soldiers and their officers lording it over them, that even the exploited English proletariat are their oppressors.

And it is true at least that the English organized workers merrily ship munitions and men across the channel for the shooting of their Irish brothers. Last Spring, following on a little propaganda and agitation, some London railmen refused to haul munitions that were going to Ireland. They had acted on the orders of Cramp, the strong man of their . union. But the railroad directors made threats and appealed to Lloyd George, who grew truculent. J. H. Thomas, the secretary of the Railwaymen's union, intervened and the order was gracefully rescinded. As usual, Thomas found the way out that was satisfactory to the moral conscience of the nation. It was not so much the hauling of munitions, he said, but the making of them that was wrong. The railroad workers should not be asked to shoulder the greatest burden of the workers' fight merely because they hold the key to the situation!

It is not the English alone, but also the anglicized Irish who persist in mis-understanding Ireland. Liberals and reactionary socialists vie with each other in quoting Bernard Shaw's famous "Ireland has a Grievance." Shaw was nice enough to let me visit him during my stay in London. He talked lovingly and eloquently of the beauty of medieval cathedrals. I was charmed with his clear, fine language, and his genial manner. Between remarking that Hyndman was typical of the popular idea of God, and asking me why I did not go in for pugilism instead of poetry— the only light thought that he indulged in—he told of a cultured Chinaman who came all the way from China to pay homage to him as the patriarch of English letters. And just imagine what the Chinaman wanted to talk about? Ireland! It was amusingly puzzling to Shaw! Yet it was easy for me to understand why a Chinaman whose country had been exploited, whose culture had been belittled and degraded by aggressive imperial nations, should want to speak to a representative Irishman about Ireland.

Whilst the eyes of the subject peoples of the world are fixed on Ireland, and Sinn Fein stands in embattled defiance against the government of the British Empire;—whilst England proclaims martial law in Ireland, letting her Black and Tans run wild through the country, and Irish men and women are giving their lives daily for the idea of freedom, Bernard Shaw dismisses the revolutionary phenomenon as a "grievance." Yet the Irish revolutionists love Shaw. An Irish rebel will say that Shaw is a British socialist who does not understand Ireland. But like Wilde he is an individual Irishman who has conquered England with his plays. There the fierce Irish pride asserts itself. Shaw belongs to Ireland.

I marvel that Shaw's attitude towards his native land should be similar to that of any English bourgeois reformist, but I suppose that anyone who has no faith, no real vision of International Communism, will agree with him. To the internationalist, it seems evident that the dissolution of the British Empire and the ushering in of an era of proletarian states, will give England her proper proportional place in the poHtical affairs of the world.

The greatest tradition of England's glory flourishes, however, in quite unexpected places. Some English communists play with the idea of England becoming the center of International Communism just as she is the center of International Capitalism. I read recently an article by a prominent English communist on city soviets. It contained a glowing picture of the great slums transformed into beautiful dwellings and splendid suburbs. When one talks to a Welsh revolutionist, a Scotch communist, or an Irish rebel, one hears the yearning hunger of the people for the land in his voice. One sees it in his eyes. When one listens to an earnest Welsh miner, one gets the impression that he is sometimes seized with a desire to destroy the mine in which his life is buried. The English proletarian strikes one as being more matter-of-fact. He likes his factories and cities of convenient makeshifts. And when he talks of controlling and operating the works for the workers, there burns no poetry in his eyes, no passion in his voice. English landlordism and capitalism have effectively and efficiently killed the natural hunger of the proletariat for the land. In England the land issue is raised only by the liberal-radicals, and finds no response In the heart of the proletariat. That is a further reason why England cannot understand the Irish revolution. For my part I love to think of communism liberating millions of city folk to go back to the land.

The English will not let go of Ireland. The militarists are hoping that the Irish people, persecuted beyond endurance, will rise protesting and demonstrating in a helpless and defenceless mass. Then they can be shot down as were the natives of Armitsar in India. But against a big 'background of experience the generals Of the Irish Army are cautious. The population is kept under strict discipline. The systematic destruction of native industries by the English army of occupation forces them to adopt some communist measures for self-preservation. They are imbibing the atmosphere and learning the art of revolution. I heard from an Irish communist in London that some Indian students had been in Dublin to study that art where it is in practical operation. It is impossible not to feel that the Irish revolution—nationalistic though it is—is an entering wedge directed straight to the heart of British capitalism.

CPSIA information can be obtained
at www.ICGtesting.com
Printed in the USA
LVHW010302250222
711939LV00004B/212

9 781528 720014